60 ONE-MINUTE
MEMORY-BUILDERS

WITHDRAWN

Other books by Dave and Claudia Arp

Ten Dates for Mates by Dave and Claudia Arp. A self-help book, containing ten fun-packed dates to boost husband-wife communication. Thomas Nelson Publishers, 1983.

Sanity in the Summertime by Claudia Arp and Linda Dillow. A survival guide for mothers to build strong relationships with their children in the summer and all year long. Thomas Nelson Publishers, 1981.

Almost 13—Shaping Your Child's Teenage Years Today by Claudia Arp. Helping you get ready for the teen years and learning how to survive them. Thomas Nelson Publishers, 1986.

MOM's Support Group Video Package by Claudia Arp. Contains a five-part video series entitled **How to Suport Your Local Parents**, and a resource guide to assist in implementing the program. Published by Marriage Alive, 1988.

MOM's & DAD's Support Group Video Package by Dave and Claudia Arp. Contains a five-part video series, leader's resource guide and ten study guides for individual participants. Published by Marriage Alive, 1989.

60 ONE-MINUTE MEMORY-BUILDERS

Dave and Claudia Arp

Wolgemuth & Hyatt, Publishers, Inc.
Brentwood, Tennessee

Wolgemuth & Hyatt, Publishers, Inc., P.O. Box 1941, Brentwood,
Tennessee 37027.

Printed in the United States of America.

Library of Congress Cataloging-in-Publication Data

Arp, Dave.
    60 one-minute memory-builders / Dave and Claudia Arp. — 1st ed.
    p.   cm.
ISBN 0-943497-51-5
1. Family—United States—Miscellanea. 2. Family festivals—
United States—Miscellanea. 3. Family—United States—Folk-
lore—Miscellanea. I. Arp, Claudia. II. Title. III. Title: Sixty
one-minute memory-builders.
HQ536.A76   1989
646.7'8—dc19   89-5490

To our three sons,
Jarrett, Joel, Jonathan.
Thanks for the unique
memories you have given us.

CONTENTS

ACKNOWLEDGMENTS

Any attempt to list all who gave input would be incomplete. However, we especially want to acknowledge and express appreciation to the following:

Thanks to David and Vera Mace, who have been wonderful teachers and mentors and have modeled to us what a growing and healthy marriage looks like!

Thanks to the Association of Couples in Marriage Enrichment, founded by the Maces, and the ACME monthly publication that gave seed for many of our Minute-Builders. (For information about ACME write to P.O. Box 10596, Winston-Salem, NC 27108.)

Thanks to Paul and Leslie Lewis and their publication *Dad's Only* that has over the years fed good ideas for family fun to us and now on to our readers. (For information about *Dad's Only* write to P.O. Box 340, Julian, CA 92036.)

Thanks to Robert Wolgemuth and Mike Hyatt, our editors who expanded our horizons and encouraged us to pass our minute builders on to you!

Thanks to Lynne Attaway for her expertise and help in editing this series.

And thanks to our three sons, Jarrett, Joel and Jonathan for being our human "guinea pigs" and allowing us to share our family memories with you.

We'll never forget those few weeks before Joel left home for college. It was summertime, but the living was anything but *easy*. Our goal that summer was to have one more family vacation, but the harder we tried to work things out, the more difficult the scheduling became.

Jarrett, our college junior, just home from Airborne School, had a job as a driver at a local car dealership. Jonathan, entering ninth grade, was busy with tennis tournaments. Joel, the college freshman, was trying to squeeze the last few pennies out of his maintenance job at the tennis club—while recovering from *mono* and getting ready to leave for college. And we, as parents, were trying to figure out how to provide our boys with one more family memory—but nothing was working! Finally in desperation, we called a family caucus. We had lowered our sights and were now trying to find one 24-hour period when all of us could break away for a mini-vacation. Even that was not coming together.

Jarrett finally asked, "What's the big deal? Why is it so important to you that we do this?" We explained that we wanted to build one more family memory before Joel officially left home.

Joel answered, "Mom, Dad, do you know how many memories we have? We have memories on top of memories! I don't need more memories to take with me—I have memories up to here!" Slowly, it began to sink in—our attempt to build more memories through a family vacation was not going to work! The major memory-building time for our family was history. Gone were the golden opportunities and moments of childhood. Our boys were moving into adulthood. We were glad that they had an abundance of good memories to take with them. We all desire that someday our children will leave home with their share of good memories. No one would say their goal is to build no memories! But life can be so busy and complicated; we can have good intentions and simply lack the time to carry them out! Some make the mistake of only looking for large blocks of time to build memories. But in today's rat race that time may not be found! Building memories does take time—but it doesn't necessarily take large blocks

of time! Family vacations are great when we can pull them off. But the majority of memories we cherish as a family happened in the little bits of time—like the time we had popcorn for breakfast or cashed in summer coupons for Just-You-and-Me Times or adopted our family puppet called Hans.

Because we all have some time—however little—and because it's not always easy to know how to use it, we've put together this little book of minute memory-builders to help you use the time you do have. Now obviously, our minute memory-builders may take more than a minute The key is they don't take lots of time and they are easy to do! Most of our memory-builders are from the Arp Family Archives and are things we actually did as a family. Obviously, we remember them! But be forewarned, as you begin to use our book, we did these things over a family lifetime. Don't try to do them all the first week—you'll end up hating us! We suggest that you use this book once a week or twice a month. It is not a book to read straight through, but instead is a resource of simple, easy, and quick ideas that you can use to add to your family's fun and storehouse of memories.

So whether you're a couple, single parent, guardian, grandparent, aunt, or uncle—whatever your situation—let us encourage you, start today and use the little moments you do have to build memories. When your children grow up and leave home, they won't leave empty-handed. They'll have memories on top of memories—just like Joel! Believe us, it worked at our house!

PART ONE

YOU ARE SPECIAL

THE RED PLATE

One Christmas we received a much-prized gift from our special friends, the Dillows. It was a beautiful red ceramic plate that says, *YOU ARE VERY SPECIAL TODAY.* It has become one of our most treasured possessions.

When do the Arps use The Red Plate? Birthdays, Mother's Day, Father's Day. When Jonathan wins a tennis match, when Jonathan loses a tennis match, when an Arp studied hard for a test but studied all the wrong things. You get the point. We use it for special days and for days that desperately need to be special.

You can find The Red Plate in most bookstores or you can create your own. One friend loved the idea and discovered a red plate and cup at a pottery factory for $1.00. It was christened in their home the day their son had a bike accident and chipped both front teeth. Barely able to eat, he had his dinner on The Red Plate and his milk in The Red Cup.

Why not start your own Special Plate tradition? There is nothing that says your special plate has to be red. It could be blue, green, whatever color you want. One family bought a pack of red paper plates at Christmas and then used them throughout the year as the Special Plate. The point is, it is used to say "You are Special." Another family we know had the tradition of the Brave Cup. Whenever anyone took a risk or attempted something new, that family member received the Brave Cup. Whatever you do, choose some way to say to your family members, "We all think you are special."

PASS THE
FAVOR KEY

Did you ever think about the fact that we need absolutely no training to be selfish and think only of ourselves? It just comes naturally. What can we do to motivate family members to think of the other person? Why not try circulating a Favor Key?

The Favor Key can be any kind of key that you happen to have. The magic is not in the key, but in keeping it circulating. The more the key moves from person to person, the more your family members will be thinking of others.

Here's how to begin. Put everyone's name in a hat or bowl and draw out a name. That lucky person gets the Favor Key first. The family member who has custody of the key may ask any other family member to do a favor for them. If that family member does the favor, he gets the Favor Key. Then he or she can ask a favor of someone else.

The point is to keep the Favor Key in motion!

As it circulates, not only will the key holder have fun, but others will discover how good it feels to do a favor for another person. So do yourself a favor. Start a Favor Key in your family today! It'll unlock kind deeds and family fun at your house.

SECRET PALS

How would you like to have a Secret Pal at your house? Having Secret Pals is one way we have found to say to each other, "You're special and appreciated."

Providing Secret Pals is a clever way to build self-esteem in your family. Here's how it works. To emphasize how special each family member is, draw names for a Secret Pal. The idea is to do something each day for your secret pal without anyone finding out who you are. In this "me"-centered world, it's healthy to focus on doing something for someone else.

To draw names, put each one's name on a separate piece of paper. Fold the pieces and put them in a bowl or hat. Keep drawing until everyone has someone else's name, even though you may have to draw several times.

Some evidences of secret pal activity at our house have been notes and jingles left on pillows and on the refrigerator, sheets on the bed turned down and a little snack under the pillow, and a basket of clean clothes folded and left in someone's room.

Secret pals remain secret for one week, and then everyone guesses who his or her pal has been. At that point you can redraw names for the next week and continue as long as it's fun for everyone. Try it. You'll be surprised at how thoughtful your secret pal can be!

HAVE A SPECIAL PERSON'S PARTY

Our families are made up of special people, but too often we don't let them know how special they are. Why not choose one family member and have a Special Person's Party? A Special Person's Party can occur at any time. Consider the following:

- when Dad or Mom worked hard on a project for months, and it just fell through

- when the neighborhood kids laughed at your child because of her new braces and she says she's not smiling for two years

- when your child studied hard for his exam but studied the wrong things

- when your teenager tripped and sprained his ankle two days before the big tennis tourna-

ment (football, soccer, basketball, dance re-
cital . . .)

- for no reason at all, but you have a small
  block of time to pull it off

You may want to plaster the walls with home-
made posters, make the honoree's favorite meal or dessert, give silly gag gifts or coupons that say, "I'll
wash your clothes for you this week," or, "I'll make
your bed for five days." Let your imagination run
wild, or better yet, ask your children—their imagi-
nations are already wild! Whatever you do, your
special person will enjoy being the "Star of the
Hour." And next time the party just may be for
you!

FIVE

SHARE YOUR STRENGTHS

One way to strengthen your own family is to share strengths with one another. Too often we dwell on the negative qualities in each other instead of searching out the positive qualities. To help you concentrate more on the positives, why not share your strengths? You'll want to find a block of time when you can all be together. That may be the hardest part, but do persevere—it's worth it. Give a card and pencil to those who are old enough to write. For younger members, oral answers will be fine.

Have each family member write down one thing they appreciate about each person in the family. Then take turns in sharing your insights with each other. You'll be surprised how good it can feel to hear your family making positive comments to one another.

You also may be surprised at what you hear. Once as we were sharing our strengths, one of our sons thanked Claudia for being an "Emotional Pit Stop."

To extend your Sharing Your Strengths time, you can include questions like:

- what is the greatest strength I bring to our family team?

- the thing I like best about our family is. . . .

Here's the good news. As you affirm your family, you'll also be affirmed in the process!

SELF-ESTEEM PASSPORT

Would you like to give your child a passport to good self-esteem? It would be silly to say no, wouldn't it? Building self-esteem in our children is not always an easy task.

To help in this area, we suggest giving your child a self-esteem passport. Here's how.

Start by looking at different areas in your child's life. Talk about each area with your mate, and together decide to help your child get the praise he or she needs.

Now to the actual passport. Here are some things you can include. Discuss these areas with your child and write down your insights in the self-esteem passport.

1. "How am I an original?" What's special and unique about me?

2. "Where do I need to grow?" List areas to work on like studies, relationships, skills, sports. . . .

17

3. "How do I show personal courage?" What risks has your child taken? Affirm him or her for that action.

4. "How have I demonstrated self-confidence?" Endorse your child's achievements. You may want to list them.

5. "How is my sense of humor?" Affirm your child for being able to laugh and look at the lighter side of things.

6. "What does it mean to say that I am a child of God?" Help your child affirm awareness of and relationship with God.

7. "What answered prayers have I seen in my life?" Make a list of answered prayers.

As parents we can do much to help our children get their needed affirmation. Maybe a self-esteem passport is a starting place for you today. Remember, a passport of good self-esteem and faith in God can take your child far in the trip of life!

ADOPT A COMMUNICATION CENTER

Do you have a communication center in your home? For us, our communication center has always been our refrigerator door. (There may be a connection as two of our favorite activities are eating and talking!) A communication center can be wherever or whatever you want—one family we know uses a chalkboard. A bulletin board with thumbtacks also works. The key is to put the center where everyone will see it and use it.

If you want to follow our example, all that you need to turn your refrigerator into a communication center are some magnets, note pads, and a little creativity. What goes on our refrigerator? Anything and everything, like:

- notes and messages

- special snapshots and memories

- cartoons and jokes (Jarrett, our law student, likes to add political cartoons whenever he's home for a visit.)

- special proverbs, verses, and sayings

- newspaper clippings

- any other message that is of interest

Here is one caution. Any communication center can become old and outdated. Always be on the lookout for new items to add. Make it fun, and it'll be one family communication tool you'll be glad you adopted!

PART TWO

ANY-TIMERS

JUST-ME-AND-YOU TIMES

Did you ever stop to think that relationships are built in twos? With a little planning, we can include special times of building twosome relationships with our children. We want to tell you about an Arp tradition, Just-Me-and-You Times.

These times are for Mom or Dad to be alone with just one child. That's when relationships are really built. We used to make the mistake of doing most things with the Arp gang—after all they were all boys and had similar interests. Group activities are great, but you only get to know someone to a certain point in a group.

How well do you know your children? What's your child's favorite color? Most loved game? Favorite food or hardest subject? To get to know your child better why not start the tradition of Just-Me-and-You Times at your house?

This may be something you would want to do weekly; if you have lots of children, maybe every other week or monthly is more realistic. The point is to do it!

Here is one word of caution. With older kids and teens you just may have to wing it. Look for those open gates and communication times. It may be at the least convenient times, like late at night or when you're tired, but grab the time when it occurs.

Take time to get to know your children. You'll be the winner, and your kids will be your friends for life!

FAMILY NIGHT

What do the words Family Night conjure up in your mind? Many parents may think of the time they tried Family Night and it was a real bomb! No one would fit into your plans and program! Or maybe you're thinking, "Family Night—that's something we really should start having in our family." Or, "Don't suggest one more thing for us to do. You just don't know my schedule!"

Hold it right there. We have no intention of adding to your family burden or guilt, but we do want to add to your family fun! Whatever your past experience has been, let us suggest a different kind of Family Night—the kind that builds memories!

Here are some simple guidelines for pulling off memory-building family times:

1. Don't overstructure your family time! It's great to have a track to run on, but no one likes to be ordered exactly what to do and how to do it! Remember, our children are in school five days a week, and their time is very structured.

They won't be that excited about Family Night if it resembles a family school.

2. Be flexible! You may have chosen your favorite game to play when everyone else is in the mood to read the book you just bought. Relax! You can trust the group, so lower your sights and go with the flow.

3. Consider your objectives. While Family Night may be an excellent time to work on instilling values and teaching spiritual truths, remember what your objectives are. We wanted to build strong relationships and strengthen our own family unit. Just plain fun was a high priority for us.

4. Know your audience! Timing is everything. A six-month-old baby doesn't exactly get into Family Night. Neither do budding adolescents! But preschool and early elementary years are great soil for planting super family memories through the vehicle of Family Night.

5. Relax. Everything doesn't always have to be perfect or work out the way we want it. The good comes with the bad. Just mop up the tempera paint from the floor and continue.

6. Do it now! Time goes by quickly. No longer is Family Night a function at the Arps. Capture the moments now, and we'll guarantee you'll enjoy the memories in the future!

PICK A
FAMILY MOTTO

Is there a phrase that describes your family—or that you wish did? If your answer is yes, why not do something about it? Why not choose a family motto? We always felt that if we said the same thing enough times, it might actually affect our family perspective. Like when the Arp brothers were ganging up on each other and seeing who could come up with the best and most sarcastic "cut-down," we reminded them of one of our family mottoes:

In our family we build each other up. There are plenty of people out there who will tear us down!

We found things got so desperate at times, we needed more than one motto! When parent-adolescent tugs of war were developing, we shot out another family motto:

Home is where you prepare for the battle, not fight it!

When things were becoming a little too serious, another favorite Arp motto came into play:

> Every family needs a little insanity to keep its sanity.

Why not take some time with your family and come up with a motto that describes (or that you would like to describe) your family? In Proverbs we are told that "as a man thinks in his heart so is he." As you affirm your family through family mottoes, you may discover that your mottoes really do describe your family!

ADOPT A FAMILY PUPPET

If you want to add to your family memory bank, consider adopting a family puppet. Puppets are great pets. They don't starve if you forget to feed them, they don't get sick or require shots, and best of all, they don't go to the bathroom on your new carpet!

In Vienna, Austria, we lived in an apartment and were not able to have a family pet other than hamsters, goldfish, and guinea pigs. (The latter we sold at a garage sale. Have you ever smelled a guinea pig?) So we adopted a puppet named Hans.

Hans was a German policeman and only spoke German. While Hans helped all of us with our German, we discovered other benefits of our adopted friend. Puppets are great for younger children who—because of embarrassment, shyness, stubbornness, or whatever reason—will not open up. It is easier for them to express themselves through a puppet than to tell you things face to face.

You can find lots of cute puppets in your local toy store or you can make your own out of fingers of old rubber gloves, socks, or sacks. (For instructions, see *Sanity in the Summertime*, pp. 75-78.) To get conversations going with your child and new puppet friend, use open-ended questions like:

- If I had three wishes, I'd wish for . . .

- The thing I like most about my family is . . .

- When I grow up, I'd like to . . .

- If I were a parent, I would . . .

- What I like best about myself is . . .

As you share experiences, answer questions, or just talk about what happened during the day with your adopted puppet, you'll be developing good communication skills as well as building memories. Ask Hans. He'll tell you we are right!

TWELVE

GOING TO NARNIA

Have you taken a trip to Narnia? If not, let us tell you how to get your travel ticket. Invest in your own set of books in the Narnia series by C. S. Lewis. Then get set for a great trip! The ideal time to visit Narnia is when your children are elementary age. That's when we traveled there. In the evening after dinner and before bedtime, we would curl up in the living room and read together aloud as Edmund, Lucy, Susan, and Peter traveled to Narnia and encountered the lion, Aslan.

That Christmas, Aslan, a lovable stuffed lion, came to live with us. He kept Narnia alive for us long after the last book was completed. Many years later, Aslan—grubby but loved—still lives in our den.

Why not invest in a trip to Narnia? You may start a family reading tradition. Some books you might consider reading aloud as a family are:

- *Little House on the Prairie* series, by Laura Ingalls Wilder (Harper)

- *Narnia* series, by C. S. Lewis (Macmillan)

- *Little Pilgrim's Progress*, by Helen L. Taylor (Moody)

- *Treasures of the Snow* and *Lost on the Trail*, by Patricia St. John (Moody)

Let us encourage you to build memories through the wonderful medium of reading together as a family.

MAKE AN APPLE TREE CHART

We have used many different tactics to motivate our children to work, and most of them did not work. If you're like us, you've already tried many charts and lists, but here is one idea that actually worked for us—for a while. It was our Apple Tree Chart. We made a green felt apple tree and three felt fruit baskets and mounted them on poster board. Each boy had his name on one basket. Then we put numbered red felt apples on the tree. We listed the jobs beside the apple tree.

For instance:

1. Set the table—if you're able.

2. The bathroom I'll clean once this week to show you that I'm really sweet!

3. To show my love, I'll vacuum the rug.

4. I'll wash the dishes all week long and do it with a happy song.

Fruit-picking time was Sunday evening. The boys "picked" apples and put them in their baskets. The next Sunday we put the apples back on the tree, and they picked different jobs for the coming week.

We wish we could say our apple tree worked indefinitely. The novelty wore off, but while it lasted, the boys were a real help. It was definitely worth the time it took to make the chart, and to this day our whole family remembers apple-picking time.

FINGERPRINT CARDS

Do you ever struggle with getting your children to write thank you notes and answer other letters to loved ones? If they design their very own cards—complete with their fingerprints—perhaps they'll be more interested in writing.

Why not help your children make Fingerprint Cards? Here's how.

Materials needed:

- Sheets of white paper or construction paper cut to make cards. (You could also use plain note paper.)

- Scissors

- Ink pad (We strongly suggest a washable ink!)

- Felt markers or crayons

How to make:

After you have cut the paper in the card shape you want, have children press their fingers one at a time on the ink pad and then on their cards. Parents or children can create flowers, bees, butterflies, or any number of designs. Use the felt markers or crayons to add stems to the flowers or wings to the bees. That's the fun part. Now if you have suggestions for getting children to sit down and write, please pass them on to us! At any rate, you'll add to your family memories.

PART THREE

MEMORY-KEEPERS

I REMEMBER

Sometimes creative ideas for memory building originate in sheer desperation. A number of years ago, Claudia found herself traveling alone with our three small children. Their international flight was turned back to New York in the middle of the night.

After a sleepless night, Claudia and the boys spent a whole day on a bus touring New York City. At last they were at the airport once again. The boys were exhausted, and Claudia was superexhausted. There was still an hour before boarding time. A belief that God would help in this desperate situation and a request to Him for wisdom and creativity resulted in the game we in the Arp family call I Remember.

Each boy thought of his day's bus tour of New York City and tried to remember everything he had seen. Then the boys took turns to see who could remember the most. Before they had finished, it was time to board the plane.

This little game helped them remember and catalog the things and places they had seen, and it left a positive impression of what otherwise could have been remembered as a real disaster day. In the years since that delayed flight, we have often played I Remember. It came in handy when we all were packed in our car like sardines, were tired, and still had hours to go. When grandparents were visiting us in Austria and getting sad about leaving, I Remember helped us all appreciate the good time we had together. Here's how to play:

Let each person take a turn and tell something different that they remember from the trip, day, event, etc. Keep going as long as anyone can come up with something new. You can play anytime you want to catalog memories:

- In the car on the way home from a family vacation

- At the end of the year, thinking back over all the things that have happened in the past twelve months

- At the end of the summer, thinking back over the past three months

- When a move is coming up

Adapt and play I'm Looking Forward To to prepare your family for the coming transition. However you adapt and use our family game, you'll have the opportunity to remember special moments that will bind you together as you face the future. This is one memory-builder you won't want to forget!

YOUR OWN ROOTS BOOK

Why not begin your own Roots book? A scrapbook, a fancy book, or an old notebook will do. Assemble several pens, pencils, stickers, and creative minds. Ask each family member to write down all the clever, ridiculous, happy, and disastrous things they can remember about themselves. Then ask them to do the same thing for the other family members. Compile the best selections in your Roots book, adding appropriate artwork or stickers. Record whatever your heart desires, such as:

- funny sayings of the children

- family happenings

- interesting news of friends and relatives

One mother of four children kept a Roots book

for sixteen years. She said it never failed to entertain them as they read about:

- Kelly, who at four sincerely thought she could fly and designed elaborate costumes for that attempt

- Stewart, who fell sound asleep on top of all the family luggage at the New York Airport

- the logical comments of Susie, who announced: "I can tie my shoes, bounce the basketball under my knees, and even blow my nose. I must be six instead of four."

Most of us haven't kept a Roots book for sixteen years, but we can begin now. It's never too late to begin cataloging memories!

YOUR FAMILY TREE

One way to give your family roots is to explore your family tree. Dave was once required to design an extended family tree called a genogram for a class. As he got into the project, we were amazed at how much family interest it created.

As we questioned older relatives about our family history, they got excited. They were pleased that we wanted to understand and know more about family members they had known and loved. We were bridging the generations. We found that one of the "ties that bind" were those twigs and branches on our family tree. To discover your own roots, why not make your family genogram? It's simple and easy to do. On a large piece of poster board, start with your immediate family and move backward. Don't forget aunts and uncles, cousins, etc. But be forewarned: you may discover a skeleton in the closet; all families have them.

Let the children interview older relatives. You may want to take notes or record or even videotape the interviews. Be prepared for lots of fun, surprises, and renewed relationships as you branch out into your family tree. You'll find a new appreciation for the future as you discover your roots in the past. We guarantee it'll be a fun memory-builder for the whole family!

FAMILY
SLIDE SHOW

It was a cold, rainy, dreary weekend. Dave was away on business, and Claudia was home with all three boys, whose energy level did not match the weather. The prospect of a whole weekend in our apartment was not thrilling to a mom who was already tired from the hectic week just passed. Out of a sense of desperation, our favorite family slide show was born!

Since Father's Day was approaching, the Arp gang decided to assemble a slide show as a surprise present for Dad. Starting back in our pre-marriage days and continuing with the birth of each child, our slide show began to take shape. An accompanying audio tape captured the magic moments as each boy narrated his birth and early years. It turned out to be such a fun project that we hardly noticed the rain outside. We heartily suggest that you consider producing your own Family Slide Show, and we'll help you to get started.

Materials needed:

- Slides of family, perhaps of children from birth to present, summer vacations, friends, relatives, places you've lived, places you've visited

- Paper and pen

- Slide projector

Activity:

- Let the children go through the slides and pick out the ones they want.

- Together, arrange the slides to tell a story of your family.

- Write a script (the funnier, the better) to go with the slides. Let the children do as much of the creative thinking and writing as possible.

- Record the script on an audio cassette tape. Add background music if you want to make it "professional." Don't forget credits at the end!

- Later, as a special family time, have the premiere showing of your Family Slide Show. Have the children work the slide projector and do the script. They will have a good feeling of accomplishment as they create, produce, and direct their own family show.

An Arp Postscript: Many years have passed since our Family Slide Show was written and produced, but we still pull it out from time to time to reminisce. Most recently we showed it to Laurie, Jarrett's fiancee! Life moves on at a rapid pace. Let us encourage you today to take the time to capture your family in time and space through your very own family documentary slide show! You'll thank us someday!

PUBLISH A
FAMILY NEWSLETTER

You don't have to have a publisher to publish your own Family Newsletter; you just need a little creativity. Newsletters are great ways to capture family memories and to share them with others at the same time. For many years we have published a newsletter for friends and for those involved with us in family enrichment. Now it's fun to pull out those letters and read our family history. One project we still need to do is to catalog all our newsletters in a scrapbook.

As you look through our letters, it's easy to see our boys' fingerprints. They have been our resident artists, joke tellers, news commentators, and copy editors.

Why not begin your own Family Newsletter? Consider publishing one each fall before mailboxes become overcrowded with all the holiday mail. If you have access to a computer, you can make it look quite professional. Think about including the following:

- recent accomplishments

- milestones

- biggest family goof of the year

- future plans

- cartoons and jokes

- pictures and art work

After composing your masterpiece, take it to a quick-print shop and duplicate it. File one copy away for safe keeping, and your family memories will be preserved!

CATALOGING MEMORIES

It's great to build memories as a family, but do you have a way to catalog and save them? We recently ran across some old audio tapes that were made when our boys were all preschoolers. It was fun to hear Joel once again sing "Johnny Appleseed" and to hear Jonathan say his first words! We almost missed these memories by not actively cataloging them! Take a few minutes to decide on ways you want to record your family history. If you have access to a video camera, why not interview your children or tape a skit or performance? Years ago a friend videotaped Jarrett's Eagle Scout Award Ceremony. That's a real treasure for us now.

Don't overlook simple scrapbooks. Fill them with snapshots, art work, writings, sayings, whatever you'd like to keep for posterity. Then keep at least one scrapbook out on a coffee table so that the whole family can look through it often.

Do you have a memento shelf? Printer's trays are popular for holding small remembrances. We have one in our kitchen with all kinds of memories in it—from homemade heart Christmas tree decorations to a small rock with "The wise man built his house upon a rock" painted on it by one of our boys years ago. Use your imagination, and you'll come up with your own unique ways of cataloging memories. In the future you'll be glad you did.

THIS-IS-YOUR-LIFE NOTEBOOK

To accentuate how special each child in your family is, why not make a This-Is-Your-Life Notebook? Include a section for each year, starting with birth. Include:

- snapshots

- artwork

- favorite sayings

- schoolteachers

- extracurricular activities

- accomplishments

- special celebrations

- information about friends

- special outings

• your own commentary

Then when your children are grown and settled in their own homes, present each with his or her own This-Is-Your-Life Notebook. They may be so impressed that when they have children, they will pass on the legacy of a This-Is-Your-Life Notebook to your grandchildren.

PART FOUR

MEMORY-SHARERS

SEND A COOKIE-DOUGH GIFT

Do you know someone who is confined indoors by illness or a child who just needs extra caring? Send-a-Cookies may be just what the doctor would order for encouragement. With your child, you can make the dough, package it, and mail it. The receiver only needs to add a few ingredients and—presto!—Send-a-Cookies are made. You'll be building memories not only for your family, but for the fortunate recipient as well. Just use the following recipe:

Send-a-Cookie Recipe:

For two batches—you can send both or send one and keep one.

- 2½ cups flour
- 3½ cups quick cooking oats
- 1¼ teaspoons salt
- 1 cup chocolate chips
- 1 cup packed brown sugar
- 1¼ Tsp. soda

- 1½ cups white sugar
- 1⅓ cups shortening
- 1 cup raisins

Stir together the flour, soda, and salt; stir in sugars. Cut in the shortening until blended. Thoroughly stir in oats. Makes about ten cups. Measure half of mix (about five cups) into plastic bag; add ½ cup chocolate chips and ½ cup of the raisins; close bag tightly. Put the remaining mix, raisins and chocolate chips into another bag and close tightly.

To mail: send it in a container which can be sealed up well, like in a plastic sack, and then a box. Include the following instructions on how to bake.

How to Bake:

Empty one bag of the cookie mix into a bowl. With a strong spoon, make a hole in the center. Into the hole drop one egg, ⅓ cup milk, ½ tsp. vanilla. With a spoon or fork mix the liquid ingredients into the dry ingredients. Drop by teaspoons a few inches apart on an ungreased cookie sheet. Bake in a preheated oven of 350 degrees for 12 to 15 minutes. One bag of mix makes about 4½ dozen cookies.

FAMILY SERVICE PROJECT

In our fast-paced world, it's not always easy to emphasize within our families the importance of serving others. It's a noble goal for our families to teach the joy of doing something for someone else without any thought of reward or recognition. Let's look at something we can do as a family to reach out to others and build memories at the same time. Consider choosing a family service project.

Begin by discussing as a family the idea of a family service project. There are many things we can do. Consider the following and choose one which seems best suited to the time and resources of your family.

1. Offer to help an elderly neighbor with some yard work. You might choose a job that he or she would have great difficulty doing alone.

2. Maybe you would enjoy becoming a support family to a child in an orphanage or children's

home. You could invite the child into your home from time to time or perhaps provide spending money and some special things like clothing or records.

3. You might choose an ecology project. You could check with city authorities and agree to de-litter a park area. Be sure to wear protective gloves.

4. Have a family cookie baking night, and send the cookies to a serviceman or college student from the neighborhood.

5. A last suggestion is to provide transportation to the store, church, or doctor's appointment for a family or person in the neighborhood.

Add your own suggestions to our list and get busy. You'll find that as you do a service project for someone else you'll also be doing a service for your own family!

SEND-A-STORY

One of the most creative gifts our family ever received was an unfinished story! It was the story of three princes and their desperate attempt to rescue their parents, the king and queen, who had been kidnaped. The three princes' personalities paralleled those of our three sons, and you can guess who the king and queen were supposed to be. Included were three small gifts for the Arp princes—clues and props to be used in completing the story. We had a great time as together we thought of the ending to the story.

Here is what you do to send a story from your family.

1. Choose a family you love and want to remember.

2. Discuss with your family the unique characteristics of each child in the chosen family and pick out one special thing about his or her personality that you could weave into a story of your own.

3. Look through your house for little things you could use as gifts and weave them into the story—pencils, rocks, toy boats, planes, or cars. You can use anything. The limit is your imagination.

4. Discuss and create a plot using your friends' personalities in the story. Get the story going, and then leave it unfinished for them to continue.

5. Write it out on paper—you can scorch it around the edge to make it look old. Or you can record the story on a tape.

6. With your kids, wrap each present and the story separately. Prepare for mailing. Take your package to the post office and send it on its way.

7. Return home for cookies and juice and lots of fun speculating on what your friends will say and on possible ways they might conclude the story when they get your special package!

SEND A CARING BOX

Do you want to help your children focus on doing something for others? Consider sending a Caring Box. Choose someone who lives in a foreign country—a missionary, a Peace Corps volunteer, or someone in the military or diplomatic service—where American goodies are not readily available. If you don't know anyone personally, check with your church or a local agency for a name and address.

Start by finding out about the needs of your chosen family. Do they live in central Africa where chocolate would melt before it arrives? Do their children read yet? Are they longing for American treats like JELL-O, chocolate chips, or pizza mix, or do they want to eat only natural foods? Do they have to pay duty, a tax, on gifts they receive? Young children might enjoy paint-with-water books, paints, brushes, puzzles, or small games. Older children probably would enjoy books. Check about Mom and Dad. Christmas music on cassette tape or a small bottle of perfume might be a welcome addition to the box.

Let the children help to wrap the box and prepare it for mailing. Then together take the package to the post office, and send it on its way.

Just think about the excitement to come as it is received by the overseas family.

On the way home stop for a milkshake or ice cream, and as you enjoy your snack, talk about the verse that says it's more blessed to give than receive. It'll be hard to decide who will be more blessed—you or the overseas family.

PART FIVE

RAINY-DAY REMEDIES

RAINY-DAY CHEST

With rainy days and bad weather, too often boredom comes along too. What can you do to keep excitement and adventure alive at your house? Why not start the tradition of a Rainy-Day Chest?

Fill a chest or trunk with small, inexpensive games and toys. Wrap each one in Sunday newspaper comics or other colorful paper. Then on rainy days when boredom strikes, open the chest and let each child pick one rainy-day surprise. Our rule was only one surprise per rainy day. You can choose a surprise time and let the children anticipate the fun they will have when they get to choose and unwrap their surprises.

Rainy-day surprises don't have to be expensive. It's much better if they are not. Actually you can probably find lots of little surprises right in your own home.

Here are some suggestions:

- materials for making your own greeting cards

- inexpensive books

- bubble-blowing liquid

- pickup sticks

- paper dolls

- marbles

- puzzles

- materials needed to make a creative collage (see pgs. 69-70)

- audio cassette tape story (This could be one you already have, but has been out of circulation for a while.)

With a little creativity and preparation, rainy days can become memory-builders at your house as you begin the tradition of your family Rainy-Day Chest.

CREATIVE CLAY DAY

Children of all ages (even parents!) enjoy the sensation of working with modeling clay, and the product is limited only by age, time, and creativity. Here are two economical recipes you can make at home.

Creative Clay:

- 1 cup cornstarch
- 2 cups baking soda (1-pound package)
- 1¼ cups cold water

Stir the cornstarch and baking soda together. Mix in cold water and stir over medium heat until the mixture has the consistency of mashed potatoes. Turn onto a plate and cover with a damp cloth until cool enough to handle. Then knead. Use immediately or store in an airtight container. This dough has a smooth consistency.

This recipe is good for ornaments, modeling, or simple pottery. It can be rolled thin and cut with cookie cutters. It will dry at room temperature in three days, or you can dry it in a 200-degree oven.

Favorite Play Dough:

- 2 cups flour
- 2 tablespoons salad oil
- 4 teaspoons cream of tartar
- food coloring

Cook over medium heat until a soft, lumpy ball forms. It happens quickly! Knead for a few minutes until dough is smooth. Store in an airtight container. The dough can be frozen and refrozen several times.

Other helpful hints to make your Creative Clay Days successful:

- A coffee can lined with a plastic bag makes a good storage container for dough.

- A recipe with no oil in it will dry hard and can be painted with tempera.

- If you leave the food coloring out while mixing, it can be added as you play.

- Adding a flavor extract like lemon or vanilla will make the dough smell good.

- Varnish or shellac a finished project to preserve it.

CREATIVE COLLAGE

Rainy days don't have to take the sunshine out of family fun. Why not make a collage? It's great if you've thought ahead to rainy-day activities, but if not, here's what you can do. Go on a scavenger hunt and see what you can find to cut and glue.

You could look for things like:

- egg noodles

- spaghetti

- macaroni

- kidney or pinto beans

- cereal with shapes

- aluminum foil

- straws

- toothpicks

- raisins or nuts

- buttons

- yarn

The list could go on and on. You can use anything that will adhere to glue, so be creative.

You'll also need glue and paper. Construction paper is great, but anything will do—like paper plates. Place all "glueable" items in the center of the table. Squeeze a small amount of glue into a paper cupcake holder for each child. Then let them create their own masterpieces!

In the evening when all the family is together, have an art show for all to see.

AGGRESSION
COOKIES

What do you do when you've planned a fun outside day and you wake up to the monsoon rains? Children know when "Go play outside" is not an option. There is no energy crisis for them, and their motto for the day is, "We're bored; there's nothing to do." This is a great time to let your kids make Aggression Cookies!

Aggression Cookies yield 15 dozen. (You might want to cut the recipe in half unless you want to feed an army!) Preheat the oven to 350 degrees.

Combine:

- 6 cups oatmeal
- 3 cups brown sugar
- 3 cups margarine
- 3 cups flour
- 1 teaspoon baking soda

Mash, knead, and squeeze "until you feel better" and until there are no lumps of margarine.

Next, form the dough into small balls, not quite as big as a walnut, and put them on an ungreased cookie sheet. Butter the bottom of a small glass and dip it into granulated sugar. Use this to flatten each ball of dough, dipping the glass into the sugar each time you press a cookie. Bake for 10-12 minutes.

Remove when lightly brown, cool a few minutes, and crisp on a rack. Store in a tight container. The dough keeps well in the refrigerator.

PART SIX

BOREDOM PREVENTERS

DO THE UNEXPECTED!

Family memories are built when we do the unexpected. Is someone in your family tired and discouraged? Why not give him or her a closet full of balloon encouragers?

Here's what we did once for Joel. It was his senior year in high school, and he was suffering from a severe case of *senioritis*. Claudia stuffed his closet with multicolored balloons. Imagine his surprise when he opened the door and a closet full of balloons floated out at him! If you want to be extra clever, you can write encouraging notes on each balloon.

Another day in his room Joel found a plate of magic cookies with the following note: "Warning! If consumed, these magic cookies will result in a desire to study, to do a research paper, and to finish college applications."

Let us encourage you! Don't take everything so seriously. Develop a sense of humor and loosen up.

Do the unexpected and expect more fun at your house!

BREAKFAST
À LA CANDLELIGHT

Most children are fascinated with matches, candles, and any open flame. Our boys were no exception. One of the first things our boys learned to do was to blow out candles.

We use candles often. Once while the family lived in Vienna, Austria, we were away, and our boys were home with a sitter. An aunt from Savannah, Georgia, came to Vienna on a tour with several of her friends. One afternoon they visited our boys. Desiring to be good hosts, our boys lit every candle in our apartment! We heard that our apartment resembled a mausoleum.

As much as we enjoyed using candles, we never considered using them at breakfast until we visited our Danish friends in Copenhagen, Denmark. To our surprise, we ate breakfast by candlelight. After returning home, we began the candlelight-at-breakfast tradition. We didn't light candles every morning, but often we did. We found that if we added pleasant music in the background, we all started the day in a much better mood. This especially worked with our sleepyheads, who aren't morning people.

Let us add one caution. Do not use unattended candles with very small children. They are too fascinated with the flame and can burn themselves or even start a fire!

So with a watchful eye, go on and enjoy a candlelight breakfast at your house. It'll wake up your sleepyheads!

THIRTY-TWO

TREASURE-HUNT
DINNER

Everyone loves to think about hidden treasures and most of us have dreamed about finding some. Here's a memory-builder that will translate a treasure-hunt fantasy into reality for your children.

Why not have a Treasure-Hunt Dinner? Plan a simple meal with lots of finger foods and things that are easy to hide like carrots, bananas, rolls, or celery sticks. Hide them in various places in your home, in drawers and closets or under the furniture. Divide the meal into courses, and after each course leave a clue to lead your children to the next part of their meal. If you want to be clever, write each clue in a jingle, like:

To discover your next food pouch, look somewhere near a couch.

Give one clue to start the treasure hunt. Have your hunters eat each course as they discover it. Before the hot course, like hot dogs (keep it all simple!), let the clue direct your children to get their baths and put on their pajamas. Then they can finish with a clue for dessert which could be a hidden cookie.

After your Treasure-Hunt Dinner, the children are ready for bed, and soon Mom and Dad can have a treasured meal alone, complete with can-dlelight, music, and conversation. If you are a single parent, treat yourself to your own favorite meal, curl up with a good book, or arrange for a baby-sitter beforehand, and go out for the evening with a friend. Whatever your situation, you can be assured that you have added to your children's storehouse of memories!

HAVE A TAFFY PULL

If you have a hankering to recreate an old-time family memory-builder, and have some old-fashioned family fun, have a taffy pull! You'll want to be sure to have a family member with a reasonably stout pair of arms or a teenager or two who want to work on building up their muscles. A taffy pull is guaranteed to drain little ones of their energy. The secret is to get them to pull and pull and pull.

For brave and strong families, here's our favorite taffy recipe.

Vanilla Taffy
- 1¼ cups sugar
- ¼ cup water
- 2 tablespoons mild vinegar
- 1½ teaspoons butter

Cook these ingredients quickly, without stirring, to just between the very-hard-ball and the light-crack stages, 268-270 degrees.

Add:

- ½ teaspoon vanilla or other flavoring

Pour the candy on a buttered platter and let it cool until a dent can be made in it when it is pressed with a finger. Gather it into a lump and pull it with fingertips until light and porous. Pull any desired flavoring or coloring into the candy. Roll it into long, thin strips and cut them into 1-inch pieces. Place the candy in a tightly covered tin if you want it to become creamy (Irma Rombauer and Marion Becker, *Joy of Cooking* [Indianapolis: The Bobbs-Merrill Company, Inc., 1964], 734).

Let us caution you: Taffy retains heat. Be careful not to burn yourself or let children begin pulling it while it's still too hot. You'll want to grease your hands before you begin to pull. For more tips about taffies and other recipes, refer to your cookbook. And don't forget to have fun!

POPCORN
FOR BREAKFAST

Are you in a breakfast rut? After all, there are just so many different breakfast menus, right? No, wrong! Why not serve popcorn for breakfast? We promise you, this is one memory-builder your family will long remember.

Several years ago, Claudia did this, and our family is still talking about it. It is hard to come up with exciting breakfast menus, and for many of us, it's just not our best time of day. We'll never forget the morning the Arp crew gathered around the table and confronted a big, huge, humongous bowl of popcorn. At each place setting was a small bowl, and on each face was confused amazement. This time Mom had really flipped.

Mom explained that because popcorn is corn and most breakfast cereals come from corn, they should think of it as having cereal for breakfast. We don't recall if we finished off that big bowl of popcorn cereal, but we do remember Joel's parting comment that morning: "Gee, Mom, I think we should have a strange breakfast at least once a month!"

None of us will soon forget our strange breakfast. In the meantime, the boys are hoping for a breakfast of chocolate chip ice cream. Who knows? One of these days, they just may get their wish!

MYSTERY MINI-VACATION

How would you like to take your family on a mystery mini-vacation? Here is one way to break the routine in your home with a mini-vacation. Start by thinking of unusual places you've never visited. You could choose a subject your family might be interested in knowing more about and make it a family field trip. Mystery mini-vacations don't have to be expensive. Why not set a $10 limit? Discover how much fun the family can have on a grand budget of ten bucks!

Or take a one-meal vacation. See how many things you can do in your local area over a time period limited to one meal out. Begin right after breakfast, eat lunch out, and be back in time for a late dinner. To add to the suspense, keep your destination a mystery as long as possible.

Here are some suggestions of possible places you could visit. What about stables where horses are trained? You may want to go horseback riding as well. Consider visiting a fire lookout tower in a protected forest. You could climb to the top and enjoy the view. Or a fish hatchery, aquarium, or nursery could be interesting places to visit. Our children always loved trips to the airport. You can go out on the observation deck and watch the planes land and take off. Consider the newsroom of a local paper or the newborn viewing room of a hospital.

If you are really brave, visit a pet store, but be sure to take along your willpower or you may come home with a new pet. At any rate, we can assure you, you'll come home with some new memories to add to your family treasures.

STINKY PINKY

Tucked away in our family memory archives are several games we used to play, but the one that we all think of first is Stinky Pinky. Stinky Pinky, a rhyming word game, is great for helping the miles go by quickly as you travel in the car or anytime boredom threatens. Stinky Pinky is appropriate for all ages, including adults. Actually we learned to play this game at an adult Sunday school party! The little tots enjoy listening and taking their turn too—although with them the rules must be modified or ignored.

Here's how to play: One person thinks of two words that rhyme, like *green bean*. Then two clues are given. The first clue is the number of syllables in each word—this is where the name of the game comes in. If the mystery words have two syllables each, then it is a *stinky pinky*. If the mystery words only have one syllable each, it is a *stink pink*. Three syllables each makes it a *stinkety pinkety*.

If one person has chosen *green bean*, he would first give this clue: "I'm thinking of a stink pink." The second clue is two words that describe the mystery words. For *green bean*, the clue could be *colored vegetable*, so the person would say, "I'm thinking of a stink pink, and it is a colored vegetable." Then the others must guess until someone comes up with the correct rhyming words. The person who guesses it right gets the next turn. To get you started, here are some suggestions:

Clue	*Stink Pinks*
cooked bread	roast toast
animal container	fox box
great dad	top pop

Clue	*Stinky Pinky*
capable furniture	able table
improved wrap	better sweater
Clue	*Stinkety Pinkety*
focused learning	concentration education
Clue	*Stinkety Pinky*
mixed-up intersection	malfunction junction

Roget's New Pocket Thesaurus can be a valuable help. So the next time you hear, "I'm bored. There's nothing to do," introduce Stinky Pinky to your family. It just may add to your memory archives!

PART SEVEN

RITES OF PASSAGE

TEENAGE CHALLENGE

Do you have an almost teen at your house? If your answer is yes, we have a great memory-builder for you! All three of our boys entered their teen years through the avenue of the Teenage Challenge.

The summer before each of our boys turned thirteen, we gave them a challenge to help them prepare for their teenage years.

We divided their teenage challenge into four goal areas—physical, spiritual, intellectual, and practical. We thought about the different areas and decided on challenges that would help to strengthen and encourage them. They were individually designed for each boy. Here are some of the things we included.

Under physical goals we had items like: run a mile in under eight minutes. Jarrett had a swimming challenge while Jonathan worked on his tennis game.

Spiritually we had them work through a code of conduct Bible study and come up with their own code of conduct for their teenage years. The one we used is found in the appendix of *Sanity in the Summertime* (Thomas Nelson Publishers).

For an intellectual challenge, each read a missionary biography and gave a report.

For the practical goal, each earned a certain amount of money, and what they saved until their birthday, we matched. All three accepted their challenges and entered their teen years a little more prepared and a little more confident. If you have a soon-to-be teen you'll find more details in the book *Almost 13* (Thomas Nelson Publishers).

Why not give your soon-to-be teen a challenge? It can be a great way to enter Teenageville both for parents and teen!

BUILDING BIRTHDAY TRADITIONS

Is it birthday time at your house? What can we do to make family members feel special on their birthdays? Birthdays at the Arp house used to be hit-or-miss. We wanted to make each birthday person feel special, but we had no plan or birthday traditions. So we decided to do something about it. Here are some of the traditions we've tried over the years. Most—but not all—have survived the passing of time. One birthday tradition we started was serving the birthday person breakfast in bed. Recently one of our son's had Swedish Pancakes à la bed. The birthday child gets to plan the menu—even if it is sticky! It is served in bed complete with candles.

Consider doing an annual birthday interview. On each birthday let your child tell you briefly about where he or she is in life at that moment. Tape record the feelings, memories, fun things that are happening. Add any other valuable information. Continue the tape on each birthday. Be sure to label the tape and put it up for safe keep-ing. What about giving your child a gift of prayer? Each year we make a list of things that we agree to pray for each of our sons for the next year. This is one gift that has no price tag and is an eternal in-vestment in their lives.

As our families grow up we are sometimes faced with the situation of not being together on birthdays. For our college students, we send pre-sents to their friends and get their friends to sur-prise them, arrange for a birthday cake or pizza to be delivered—whatever is needed to say, "Happy Birthday. You are special. We love you!"

We top it off with a phone call—that's if the lines are free and we can connect. Actually we keep persevering till we can give them that old line that everyone loves to hear, "Happy birthday!" Remember, birthdays come regularly and we can make them special memories!

BIRTHDAY
BOXES

Consider this. Our job as parents is to work ourselves out of a job. We wanted our sons to be able to function on their own before they left the nest, between the ages of eighteen and nineteen. Launching our children into the teen years is only the first step. Then the countdown to adulthood begins.

To help in this process, we began a process of release we called the Arp Birthday Boxes. Together we developed an overall plan. Then we broke it down into yearly responsibilities and privileges that we put in a Birthday Box and gave to each son on his birthday starting at age thirteen.

Some of the areas that we included were:

• Curfew

• Academics and homework

• Rooms

- Clothes and grooming

- Money

- Dating and parties

- Spiritual life

- Driving

- Part-time jobs

These were negotiable, but our goal was to work toward independence by age eighteen. The Rocket Ship illustrates a suggested progression. The key to getting more responsibilities and privileges was tied into how the teen handled his box. The one who showed lots of responsibility and maturity got new privileges and responsibilities sooner. Not only did our Arp Birthday Boxes help us as parents to let go, but they also communicated to our teens that we were excited that they were growing up and becoming adults.

Why not give this memory builder a try at your house? For more details, please refer to the book *Almost 13*.

STARTING A FAMILY BUSINESS

Are you looking for a way to help your children learn more responsibility? Most children look forward to that magic age of sixteen, when legally they can start a part-time job. From our experience, we've found that part-time jobs have their pros and cons and don't always add to family unity. But here's a money-making venture that does create family togetherness: Why not start a family business? A definite rite of passage in the Arp family was the year that the Arp boys bought a peanut butter business. We were living in Vienna, Austria, and peanut butter—if we could find it—was very expensive. There was a large international community in Vienna with many peanut butter lovers. One of our boys' friends was moving back to the States. He sold them his peanut butter machine and his list of customers for $25, and the Arp Peanut Brothers business was born.

This business venture proved to be an excellent way for them to develop responsibility and to see the benefits of hard work. They had to keep books and records of time spent, peanuts bought, and jars sold. Each month they received their share of the profits. Profits were directly related to the amount of time spent making peanut butter. One month, one of the boys earned only fifteen cents while his brothers earned twelve dollars and five dollars. The next month he really got with it and did his share of the work and earned his share of the profits.

We called the peanut butter business a family business because it required commitment from parents as well. We were involved in helping to shop for peanuts and driving the boys around to make deliveries. And sometimes in self-defense, we helped clean up the mess in the kitchen. Wasn't all of this a hassle? YES! Wasn't it a pain at times? YES! Was it really worth it? Emphatically, YES! Years later as Jarrett at age sixteen applied for his first official part-time summer job, he was the only applicant who produced a resume and the only one who had previously owned a business.

Why not take some family time and talk about business ventures you could start together? It could be a one-time yard sale to earn money for a special family outing or to help someone you know who has a special need. You'll find that as you venture out together, you'll help build responsibility and good memories. Good luck!

CHOOSE A HOME-IMPROVEMENT PROJECT

Do you have a project around your house that is begging to be done? Why not recruit your own family workers and build family memories as well?

Several years ago when we returned to the U.S., we moved back into our old house. Major repairs were needed, and we decided to try to do one project ourselves. For years we had talked about turning our patio into a screened porch. Now with three adolescents, it was more within our reach.

Because none of us are talented carpenters, we hired a carpenter to work with us and guide us in constructing our screened porch. Everyone was involved, from buying and delivering the materials to painting and roofing.

After two weeks we had completed our screened porch and had added lots of new memories—most of them the good kind. Since then, many memories have been added to our storehouse while we sat and talked on our screened porch. Think about home-improvement projects for your home. Maybe it's a wallpapering job or some shelves that need to be put up. Remember, some of your best workers may be under your very own roof. As you improve your home, you'll also improve your family memories!

LET'S PLANT
A TREE

Landscaping your yard can add to your family history! Is an important event coming up on your family calendar—a birthday or a special milestone? Why not celebrate it by planting a tree?

Consider the following:

- birthdays

- Christmas

- your child's first day of school

- losing a tooth

- an accomplishment like learning to ride a two-wheel bike

- any other event you'd like to celebrate and remember

Choose the spot for the memorial tree. Then visit a nursery and select one together. Or if you have access to a woods, dig your own tree. Plant the tree together. You may want to add a marker. Using a small piece of treated wood, write what the tree commemorates, like:

In honor of Megan's first day at kindergarten 8-28-88.

Years ago, our boys helped plant several trees in our yard. Then we lived out of the United States for a number of years. When we moved back, it was fun to return to our "roots" and see how much the trees had grown. In the future if you move away, go back occasionally to see how your trees have grown. You'll feel more connected to your "roots."

FORTY THREE

LEARN A NEW SPORT

When our boys were young and began to show an interest in sports, we were quick to read the handwriting on the wall. If we were to be family participators instead of family spectators, we were going to have to learn some new skills.

Dave was more athletic than Claudia, but both agreed to give it the good ol' try. We wanted to choose a sport that we could enjoy together with our children in their adolescent years and into adulthood. Since we lived in Austria, skiing was a natural—except for learning how!

We'll never forget those first attempts on the slopes. We all felt quite helpless and inept. Being on the same level—beginners—gave us a feeling of being a "team." We were determined to learn even if it involved pain and suffering.

As you probably could predict, it didn't take long for our boys to pass us up, but that also worked in our family's favor. The adolescent years are usually a time when it seems there is little our children can do right. Parents always seem to have the edge of experience. But on the ski slopes, the three Arp boys were the experts. They even occasionally slowed their pace to encourage Mom or Dad or even give us a short lesson.

If you want to get on a "even" basis with your children, look around and pick a sport you would like to learn or do together. Skiing may not be an option for you. What about tennis, jogging, racketball, or whatever?

You may never make the Olympics, but we guarantee you'll build family memories.

PART EIGHT

SUMMER SIZZLERS

FORTY - FOUR

PLANNED SUMMERS

Instead of drifting through June, July, and August, why not turn summer from mere survival into sanity by starting the tradition of planned summers? Planning can make a big difference in how your children will remember summertimes.

Here's an idea that worked for us when our children were growing up. At the beginning of the summer, we would set them down and ask these three questions.

1. "What do you want to do for fun this summer?" After we convinced them we couldn't build a swimming pool in the back yard, they got with it and made some good suggestions like a trip to the zoo, swimming, playing soccer, visiting a museum, going on a picnic, and having a party for no reason at all. We chose one day a week as Children's Day, and on that day we did fun things together—often from the list we had made.

2. "What would you like to learn this summer?" This was sometimes a new sport or skill. One nice thing about summer is that the pace of living is slower if we don't fill our days with fifteen new commitments. Planning was a great help.

3. "What can you do for someone else?" In this *me generation*, we can use all the encouragement we can get to do something kind for someone else. One friend's son offered to mow the yard for an elderly neighbor.

Let us encourage you to take the time to plan your summer. Try using our three questions with your family. You'll find that your summer will be fun and that you can experience sanity in the summertime!

FORTY - FIVE

CHILDREN'S DAY

When is an ideal time to do creative, fun activities with our children? When it's not raining and not too hot or too cold, when there is no work piled up on the desk and the phone is not ringing, when we've had ten hours of sleep—the list could go on and on. We might conclude that there is no ideal time to do fun things with our children.

To help assure that time was spent building the relationships with our boys each summer, we initiated the tradition of Children's Day. Our goal was that one of us would do one special thing with the children each week.

At the beginning of the summer, we set our boys down and asked for suggested activities for Children's Day. Then, before each Children's Day, we picked an activity from our list, like:

- take a trip to the zoo

- go swimming

- take a picnic to the mountains

- go bike riding

- have a party for no reason at all

- visit a museum

Once Claudia thought it would be fun to hold a joint Children's Day with her good friend, Linda, and Linda's three children. It was a fun day for all. Claudia and Linda enjoyed adult talk, and all the children had a great time. But thinking back on the day, Claudia realized she had not reached her objective—to spend time alone with her children. She learned that for best results, she would keep Children's Day within the family.

Lest you think every Arp Children's Day was flawless, let us clarify. Sometimes Children's Day, even with all our planning, just didn't happen. Some Children's Days were sabotaged by brothers who couldn't get along. Sometimes it rained when we had planned an outside event. But SOMETIMES things went right, and good memories were built. We recommend that you give Children's Day a try at your house.

IT'S BACK YARD
CIRCUS TIME

A re you looking for a great birthday party suggestion? Or maybe an idea for a party for no reason at all? Consider a back yard circus! Your children will enjoy being in on the planning and preparation.

The first step is to make an invitation list. With younger children, a good rule of thumb is to have one helper (older child, teen, or other parent) for every five children. For fun invitations, use felt markers to write on an inflated balloon.

Let the air out and send one to each of the guests. Ask each guest to dress as a favorite performer and to bring a favorite "wild" stuffed animal.

Decorate large cardboard boxes as cages for transporting "wild" animals. Almost anything can be used to decorate—finger paint, felt markers, tempera paints, leftover pieces of wallpaper, or contact paper. Tie a string to the front of the boxes and connect all the boxes with string. Rope off circus rings in the yard. Use rope, string, the garden hose, or whatever you can find to resemble a ring. Each ring can be a performance area for costumed guests. Let each ring perform for the other. One ring could feature singers, another acrobats or dancers, another jugglers. A happy music cassette adds to the atmosphere.

After the performance, serve animal cookies and juice. Then send your happy performers home with new and fun memories!

MY BAG
AND YOURS

How we can make family travel triumphant? Each June families all over the U.S. hit the vacation roads committed to having family fun . . . no matter how much suffering it entails. Unless you are in the minority, your summer plans will include at least one car, plane, or train trip with your children. Whether you head for grandparents, Disney World, or the unknown, you will have hours of real family closeness.

Traveling with children is usually challenging and can be exasperating, but it also can be a fun memory-building time. Here are some tips on making travel time sane. Preparation really helps! Consider taking along memory travel bags.

Take along "my own bag" for each child. Instead of an actual bag, you may want to use a metal cake pan with a sliding cover. It's excellent for holding pencils, paper, crayons, scissors, activity books. . . . You get the picture. It can also double as a writing surface. Children's bags can be filled with items they already have.

New travel treasures come from Mom's Travel Bag. "A surprise a day keeps tears and quarrels away!" (At least some of the time.) "Mom's travel bag" adds an air of expectation. If your trip is a long one, you can choose a special time each day to dip into Mom's Travel Bag or use it when things are getting boring. We've found that activity-oriented surprises are best, as they give the children something to do. Consider things like:

- magic erasable slate

- punch-out paper dolls

- doodle art

- magnetic checker set

- books

- Band-Aids—you'd be amazed at what one child can do with one box of band-aids!

And don't forget to take along a food bag—that may be the most important bag of all. For more travel tips please refer to *Sanity in the Summertime* (Thomas Nelson Publishers, Nashville).

Remember successful traveling begins before the trip begins. Travel bags can add sanity to your vacation travel plan!

MAKE A
TRAVEL NOTEBOOK

What visions fill your mind when you think of traveling with young children? One father said he felt condemned to drive his tribe across hundreds of miles filled with screams, attempted homicides, and innumerable unscheduled pit stops, as he wished the kids had taken more Dramamine and he had taken several extra-strength Excedrin! Perhaps you're just getting ready to start on a family vacation. Here's a suggestion that might make the hours in the car more fun. Anticipation can almost be as enjoyable as the trip itself. Why not spend a little time before your trip and help your children make a travel notebook?

Here are some suggestions to get you started. For each child buy a simple ringed notebook, dividers, and paper. Divide the notebook into sections. One can be interesting facts about the place you are going. You can look for information at travel agencies and in encyclopedias.

Another section could be a daily travel log. Here the child can write a brief daily diary of the trip. Include a section for postcards and other souvenirs they purchase. Remember a money section where the child can keep account of his own money and how it disappears! Be sure to include a blank section with extra sheets of paper for drawing, tic-tac-toe, or creative writing.

With a little preplanning, those hours in the car can be calm. And in the cold, cold days of winter, looking through your child's travel notebook will bring warm memories to your home!

THANKSGIVING IN JULY

How would you like to have Thanksgiving in July? Every November, we are reminded to thank God for the big things in our lives. Why not set aside July to say thanks for the little things? Why not sit down for a minute with your family and consider your situation. What little things are you thankful for?

Here are some suggestions to get you started:

- Review the last twenty-four hours and list twenty-four things, people, or experiences that have made your life more enjoyable. Then thank God for each.

- We often thank God with music, but why not for music and the way tunes run through our thoughts?

- Imagine a colorless world. Then thank God for color and sight.

- Bring to mind your most pleasurable childhood memory, and say thank you.

- What has been the high point of this week so far?

- Imagine life without a reasonably efficient postal system and thank God for ours.

Here are some other things to add to your list: the change of seasons, your favorite author, mirrors, windows, aspirin, correcting typewriter ribbons, your best friend. When you add up all the little things you are thankful for, you'll want to say a big thank you to God and all those who have blessed your life—starting with your family!

PART NINE

FALL FLAVORS

IT'S PUMPKIN TIME

Don't overlook the fun you can have with pumpkins. When our boys were younger, we grew our own pumpkins. The boys helped to plant them and had lots of fun watching them grow. Once we made the mistake of planting them in the shade. Our total crop was one miniature pumpkin about the size of a tennis ball. In real families who build real memories, everything doesn't always turn out the way they expect! The fun part is to keep trying, so take the chance and plant those pumpkin seeds!

Beside the traditional jack-o'-lantern, you can make your fall dinner table more festive by helping the kids turn pumpkins and other large gourds into serving dishes.

Just scoop out the insides, then decorate the outside by scalloping the edge or chiseling designs in the skin. Let small children decorate them with finger paints. You can serve your favorite meal from these most unusual bowls. If you happen to grow miniature pumpkins as we did, why not scoop out the center and use a pumpkin as a festive candle holder?

After creating your table decorations, get a head start on Thanksgiving and make a pumpkin acrostic. Beside each letter in the word pumpkin, list something you are thankful for, like:

Parents
Umbrellas

Many friends
Parties
Kittens
Interesting hobbies
Nice toys
Summer memories

Go ahead and let pumpkins add to your fall fun. We can assure you—you'll beat boredom at your house and build memories in the process.

FIFTY - ONE

THANKSGIVING COUPONS

When we lived in Austria, one tradition we had was always eating Thanksgiving dinner with our friends, the Dillows. One year to show our families how much we appreciated them, we made "I'm thankful for you" coupon books and used them for place cards for our family members. Included were coupons for making Christmas cookies alone with Mom, a trip with Mom to a Christmas market, and going out for a hot chocolate date. They were such a big success that we discovered we had started a tradition, as our children asked the next Thanksgiving, "Do we get another coupon book this year?"

You may not realize it, but family members are the most neglected during those four weeks between Thanksgiving and Christmas. We are so busy doing things for our family that we may overlook spending time with them. By starting the tradition of Thanksgiving Coupons, you can ensure that time is spent with each family member in the midst of busy holiday activities.

Here is how to make a Thanksgiving coupon book.

Material Needed:

- Index cards

- Cute stickers

- Hole puncher

- Yarn

- Felt markers

Instructions:

Punch two holes in cards. Decorate cards with stickers. Write out coupons for each child, using one card for each coupon. Tie each coupon book together with yarn.

Give your coupon books on Thanksgiving (or adapt for any time of year) to your lucky family members!

FIVE GRAINS
OF CORN

Five grains of corn can keep tradition alive at your home this Thanksgiving. There is an early Thanksgiving tradition that can help your family remember the real meaning of Thanksgiving.

The American Thanksgiving Day was for the Pilgrims an expression of a deep feeling of gratitude for the rich productivity of the land, a memorial of the dangers and hardships through which they had safely passed, and a fitting recognition of all that God, in His goodness, had bestowed upon them. Five grains of corn were placed at every plate as a reminder of those stern days in the first winter when the Pilgrims' food supply was so depleted that only five grains of corn were rationed to each individual at a time.

The Pilgrim Fathers wanted their children to remember the sacrifice, suffering, and hardships through which they had safely passed and the resulting freedom and privilege of settling in a free land. The five grains of corn reminded them of the sixty-three days on the tiny Mayflower—and that first terrible winter which took such a toll of lives. The grains of corn were a fitting reminder of a heroic past.

Why not use this tradition this year in our families to remind each of us of hard times of sacrifice and God's protection and provisions in the middle of trials. Press a leaf or cut one from construction paper, and on each leaf by each plate, place five grains of corn. As you begin your Thanksgiving feast, share the story of the Pilgrims and the significance of the five grains of corn.

As you talk about the five grains of corn, you could also talk about five things you are thankful for. You'll find that this tradition can serve as a useful means of recalling those great gifts for which we are grateful to God. A thankful Thanksgiving can start with five grains of corn and you!

PART TEN

WINTER WONDERS

FIFTY THREE

MAKING TRADITIONS MEANINGFUL

What special traditions do you have in your family? Traditions make you unique as a family, and, whether simple or elaborate, they become part of the fabric of your life. Stop and think about the traditions that you have carried on over the years in your family. Which ones are the most meaningful? Are there things that you continue to do that are only a ritual and no longer have real meaning? Maybe it's time to evaluate.

As a family make a list of your family's traditions. Discuss together the ones that are especially important to you.

Discuss the following questions.

- Where did a specific tradition come from— your own childhood, other families, or a magazine or book?

- Have some traditions disappeared over the years?

• Have new ones been added?

• What would your family be like if all your traditions were stripped away?

• Are there some traditions that you would like to add?

The good news is that you can stop, begin, and even begin again traditions whenever you want. Remember, family life is fluid and always changing. Begin the tradition of making traditions meaningful to your family.

FIFTY - FOUR

WHOSE BIRTHDAY IS IT?

Imagine that it's your birthday. Everyone gives gifts to one another but completely ignores you. That's what some of us do at Christmas time. We forget just whose birthday we are celebrating.

How can we help our families focus on the real meaning of Christmas? Why not have a birthday party for Jesus? When our boys were young, we actually had a birthday cake with candles and sang "Happy Birthday" to Jesus. We also gave an individual gift to Him each year. Our guidelines were that each gift was to be a gift of love, not money, and was something we would give Him of ourselves.

Each Christmas Eve, we individually wrote what our gift was on a card and put it in an envelope, sealed it, and put it on the tree. We saved the envelopes until the next year. Each year we reviewed what we had written on our cards the year before. Those who wanted to tell what they gave the previous year could speak up, but there was no pressure to speak on family members who were more private or introverted. Then we prayed together and wrote out our cards for the coming year. Some gifts our family members gave were:

- commitment to pray more regularly for our family

- lose ten pounds of overweight

- argue less with a brother

- stop biting fingernails

As our boys grew older, our Christmas birthday celebration was modified. We still have the fresh coconut cake, but without singing and candles. We still write our gifts on a card and put them on the tree, but our gifts and sharing time have become more a time of reflection and goal setting. We like to evaluate the last year and focus on the coming year by setting goals for ways we want to grow and mature. Remember, for traditions to remain meaningful, we need to modify them as necessary.

However you celebrate the birthday of our Lord, let us challenge you to make it personal, make it meaningful, and make it Christ-centered. Adapt your celebration to meet your family where they are, and center in on the real meaning of Christmas. Then, at your house, you will experience His very best!

FIFTY - FIVE

THE TWELVE DAYS
OF CHRISTMAS

Do you want to send a very unique and unusual Christmas present to a family you love? Let us tell you about a memory-building gift we received from our dear friends, the Peddicords. They sent us "The Twelve Days of Christmas." As we opened the Christmas box, the first thing we saw was a book of Christmas carols with this note:

Sing the song on page 26 before opening this present or sharing it with others. Sit together

and have time without other distractions too, if possible. We're thinking of you this Christmas! Love, Clark and Ann

You guessed it! The song was "The Twelve Days of Christmas," and in the box were twelve gifts to be opened. Each was numbered so we knew how to proceed, and each represented one of the twelve days of Christmas. Why not have some fun this year and send "The Twelve Days of

Christmas" to a family you know. Use your imagination. Here are some suggestions to get you started.

- Day 1—a partridge in a pear tree—This could be "homemade art" drawn by one of the children.
- Day 2—two turtle doves—Our friends sent a small framed picture of two birds that is still on our memento shelf.
- Day 3—three French hens—Make three chicken Christmas tree ornaments out of felt.
- Day 4—four calling birds—Draw a picture of four birds all talking on the telephone.
- Day 5—five golden rings—Make five gold napkin rings out of felt. Simply cut in strips (2″ by 6″) and sew the short ends together.
- Day 6—six geese a-laying—What about six chocolate eggs?

We've gotten you started. On the last six, you're on your own!

- Day 7—seven swans a-swimming —
- Day 8—eight maids a-milking —
- Day 9—nine ladies dancing —
- Day 10—ten lords a-leaping—
- Day 11—eleven pipers piping —
- Day 12—twelve drummers drumming—

Wrap the gifts individually, label them, and send this unique gift on its way. Be sure to include a copy of the song, "The Twelve Days of Christmas" and a note suggesting that they set aside at least thirty minutes to an hour to open and enjoy your gift. Then sit back and wait for their happy response!

MAKE YOUR OWN CHRISTMAS DECORATIONS

One of the most fun parts of decorating for Christmas is pulling out our Christmas tree decorations. Our Christmas tree has never been in the running for the *House Beautiful* award, but it might tie any family's in the category of Memories. Why not add to your Christmas storehouse of memories each year? Let your children make several new Christmas tree ornaments. As the years go by, they will become more special to you.

Our favorite ornaments have been the wax ones we have made in the shape of hearts. These were simple to make and have lasted through the years. One caution, they must be stored in a cool place or they will melt!

Supplies needed:

- old candles or wax
- crayons (to add color)
- double boiler (or can in a pan of water)

- pie tin
- cookie cutters (heart-shaped ones were our favorite)
- old oilcloth to protect table
- crochet needle
- yarn
- tempera or oil paints

Directions:

1. Place old candles or wax in a double boiler and melt. *With younger children, you should supervise closely: Melted wax can burn!*

2. Pour melted wax ¼ thick into pie tin.

3. As the wax begins to harden, cut it with cookie cutters.

4. Punch a hole in the top center of ornament.

5. When cool and firm enough to handle, remove each ornament. Put the leftover pieces of wax back in the double boiler and reuse.

6. Cut a six-inch piece of yarn. Pull it through the hole and tie it.

7. You can paint and decorate your ornaments or use them as they are. You may want to initial and date each ornament on the back.

Not only did we enjoy decorating our tree, but some years we made extra ornaments and gave them to relatives and friends. We hope you enjoy this memory-builder as much as we have!

CREATE YOUR OWN NATIVITY SCENE

Each Christmas we pull out a very special nativity scene. It would win no art contest. The little play dough figures look the worse for wear. One angel has a broken wing and her halo is lost. The camel only has three toothpick legs. The wise men have long ago lost their gifts. But it still gets center stage at our house. Why? Because it is one of our most special holiday memories and traditions.

It all started one holiday season years ago when the three boys were bored and hyper. We were temporarily living in the U.S., and our Christmas decorations, including our nativity scene, were packed away at our home in Austria. With more time than money or talent, we decided to create our own nativity scene.

Using the Creative Clay recipe on page 67, we molded our little people. They somewhat resembled little Fisher Price people, just a little more (or perhaps a lot more) rustic! We let them dry and then painted each with tempera paints. The following

Saturday we took a walk through the woods and picked up anything of interest, such as moss, roots, acorns, sticks, stones, and pine cones. We brought our "treasures" home, and on a piece of plywood, we constructed our very own nativity scene. The manger was crafted from a root covered with moss. Pine cones served as trees. The final touch was adding our little nativity people and animals that we had made from the play dough. When we returned to our home in Austria, we took our little people along. Each year we took a family walk in the woods picking up goodies, and later at home we reconstructed our manger scene. How special it has been each Christmas to bring out our little homemade nativity people—broken wings, broken legs, and all. They bring back great memories of Christmases past.

So when boredom threatens to strike at your home, pull out the play dough recipe. Make your own nativity people, take your own walk in the woods, assemble your own simple nativity scene, and add to your family's special Christmas memories.

SPRING SPECIALS

EGGSHELL GARDEN

Springtime is a time of planting and watching things begin to grow. If you live in a cold climate and it's too cold to start a garden outside, why not plant an egg shell garden? Choose whatever seeds you want to plant—beans, radish, or any fast-growing seeds. As you daily water and watch the seeds grow, you'll have lots of opportunities to talk with your children about how we grow in our lives both physically and spiritually.

Here is how to make your eggshell garden.

Material needed:

- eggshells
- seed
- potting soil
- egg carton
- container to mix soil
- popsicle sticks

How to plant: Fill the eggshells with moist potting soil. Set them in an egg carton. Plant several seeds in each shell. Plant either a variety of seeds or all of the same type. Use popsicle sticks to make labels for the different kinds of seeds. Place the egg cartons in a bright window, and keep the soil barely moist. To transplant outdoors, gently crush the eggshell and plant the seedling, shell and all.

FIFTY NINE

CROWN OF
THORNS

Are you looking for a way to celebrate the real meaning of Easter? Consider making a crown of thorns. Here's how. Use a vine with thorns or branches of a climbing rose bush or a wild blackberry plant. Shape and twist it until it resembles a crown of thorns. Discuss as a family why Jesus was willing to wear a crown of thorns and the significance it holds for each of us today.

Next make play dough using one on the recipes on pages 67-68. Divide the play dough so that each family member will have some. Let each person choose a color and work that color into the piece of play dough. Store the colored play dough in airtight plastic bags. Leave the bags by the crown of thorns. As a family, focus on what Christ has done for us, how much God loves us, and how much He loves everyone. Talk about how we can show our love for Him by showing kindness to those He loves.

Suggest that between then and Easter, each time a family member does a kind deed for someone else, he or she can take a small amount of play dough, form a berry, and cover one of the thorns on the crown of thorns. We hope that by Easter the crown of thorns will be transformed into a beautiful wreath of berries. Together thank God that He makes the rough places smooth and is the giver of new life and new beginnings!

DECORATE AN EASTER EGG TREE

Almost everyone has a Christmas tree, but have you ever had an Easter egg tree? This is an Arp tradition we adopted while we lived in Vienna, Austria. For the tree, use a branch just as it is or spray-painted white. You may also use sprigs of pussy willow or forsythia blossoms. Put them in a vase or container, and you have an Easter egg tree all ready for decorating.

Here's how to make your own egg decorations.

1. Use real eggs. Punch a small hole in both ends of a raw egg. Use an ice pick to break the yolk. Holding the egg over a bowl, blow on one end. With a little effort the yolk and white of the egg should be forced out of the other end of the egg and into the bowl. (This may be the evening to have omelettes for dinner.)

2. Paint the eggs any color that you like. A variety of colors will look attractive on your

Easter egg tree. Place the eggs in an old egg carton and let them dry.

3. Now the fun! Decorate the eggs any way you want to. You can paint designs on the eggs—hearts, flowers, or curlicues. You can use rick rack, borders, stencils, yarn, felt, or whatever you like. One year one of our boys cut out little pieces of felt and made an empty tomb on his egg.

4. Cut yarn into eight-inch lengths. Thread the yarn through a large needle and push it through the two holes in each egg. Tie a large knot in the end at the bottom so the yarn will stay and not pull through. Use the other end of the yarn to tie the egg onto the tree.

Enjoy your Easter egg tree with your family. Talk about the real meaning of Easter and how God gives new life. Each year as you pull out your Easter egg tree, you'll pull out special memories!

BIBLIOGRAPHY

Arp, Claudia. *Almost 13*. Nashville, TN: Thomas Nelson Publishers, 1986.

Arp, Claudia, and Linda Dillow. *Sanity in the Summertime*. Nashville, TN: Thomas Nelson Publishers, 1981.

Arp, Dave, and Claudia Arp. *Ten Dates for Mates*. Nashville, TN: Thomas Nelson Publishers, 1983.

Campbell, Ross. *How to Really Love Your Child*. Wheaton, IL: Tyndale House Publishers, 1982.

Dobson, James. *The Strong-Willed Child*. Wheaton, IL: Tyndale House Publishers, 1988.

Kesler, Jay. *Parents and Teenagers*. Wheaton, IL: Victor Books, 1984.

King, Pat. *How to Have All the Time You Need Every Day*. Wheaton, IL: Tyndale House Publishers, 1980.

Liontos, Lynn, and Demetri Liontos. *The Good Couple Life*. Winston-Salem, NC: The Association of Couples in Marriage Enrichment, Inc., 1982.

McGinnis, Alan Loy. *The Friendship Factor*. Minneapolis, MN: Augsburg Publishing House, 1979.

Mace, David. *Close Companions: The Marriage Enhancement Handbook*. New York: Continuum, 1982.

Mace, David, and Vera Mace. *How to Have a Happy Marriage*. Nashville, TN: Abingdon Press, 1977.

_____. *Love and Anger in Marriage*. Grand Rapids, MI: Zondervan Publishing House, 1982.

Peterson, J. Alan. *The Marriage Affair*. Wheaton, IL: Tyndale House Publishers, 1974.

Ridenour, Fritz. *What Teenagers Wish Their Parents Knew About Kids*. Waco, TX: Word Publishers, 1982.

Sell, Charles. *Achieving the Impossible: Intimate Marriage*. New York: Ballentine, 1982.

Stanley, Phyllis, and Miltinnie Yih. *Celebrate the Seasons*. Colorado Springs, CO: Nav Press, 1986.

COLOPHON

The typeface for the text of this book is a modern version of *Goudy Oldstyle*, made more suitable for text typesetting because of a tighter set and a more subtle presentation of the distinctive flourishes that characterize it. Its creator, Frederick W. Goudy, was commissioned by American Type Founders Company to design a new Roman type face. Completed in 1915 and named Goudy Old Style, it was an instant bestseller. However, its designer had sold the design outright to the foundry, so when it became evident that additional versions would be needed to complete the family, the work was done by the foundry's own designer, Morris Benton. From the original design came seven additional weights and variants, all of which sold in great quantity. However, Goudy himself received no additional compensation for them. He later recounted a visit to the foundry with a group of printers, during which the guide stopped at one of the busy casting machines and stated, "Here's where Goudy goes down to posterity, while American Type Founders goes down to prosperity." The perfect blend of beauty and versatility of this classic and graceful design adds distinction wherever it's used. It is considered the most popular advertising typeface in use today.

Copy editing by Donna Sherwood
Cover design by Kent Puckett Associates, Atlanta, Georgia
Typography by Thoburn Press, Tyler, Texas
Printed and bound by Dickinson Press, Inc.
Grand Rapids, Michigan
Cover Printing by Weber Graphics, Chicago, Illinois